Savin_

Contents

written by John Lockyer

The tiger is a beautiful animal that lives in dry grasslands, hot jungles, and snowy forests. It has a special coat to help it hide when it is hunting or sleeping.

It has long, thick, ginger fur, and its belly is white. Its head, body, tail, and legs have black or brown stripes.

Not long ago, there were about 100,000 tigers in the world. Now there are only about 5,000 left. Some kinds of tigers have become extinct.

The tiger is disappearing because the places where it lives are changing. People are cutting down trees and digging up the land for new farms, homes, and factories.

Tigers need lots of space to move around. But their grasslands, forests, and jungles have become so small that they can't find enough animals to hunt for their food.

When tigers get very hungry, they hunt everywhere for prey. Sometimes they attack cows and goats, and even people, near villages. Farmers often kill these tigers to protect their families and their animals.

farmer

Many tigers are killed by hunters called poachers, who want them for their body parts. Tiger skins are used to make rugs and coats. Medicines are made from tiger bones, and tiger claws are used on costumes.

In some countries, a few people hunt tigers for sport. Tigers are endangered animals because of hunters, poachers, and the clearing of the land where they live.

tiger cubs

Many people are trying to save the tiger. They learn all about tigers so that they can teach others how to help tigers survive.

They write letters to important people to tell them how the tiger has become endangered. These people often help to buy land for tiger reserves, too.

Tiger reserves are special places where tigers can be safe. The reserves are in jungles, forests, and grasslands. No one can hunt tigers in these places.

There are plenty of trees and plants growing in the reserves. They can't be cut down, so there is always lots of food for animals like deer, antelope, and buffalo. These are animals that the tiger hunts.

spotted deer

Trees and plants help tigers in another way. Tigers hunt by sneaking up on their prey. If they don't have enough trees and plants to hide behind, they can't catch their food.

Tigers can still be saved, but their homes and food must be saved first. Saving the tiger means saving the environment!

Can you see a tiger here? It's hiding in the trees and grasses. It has almost disappeared.
If this wonderful animal doesn't get more help, it might disappear from the world forever.